T0145051

God's Perfect Gift

Written and Illustrated by Amie Charney

WestBow Press books may be ordered through booksellers or by contacting:

WestBow Press
A Division of Thomas Nelson & Zondervan
1663 Liberty Drive
Bloomington, IN 47403
www.westbowpress.com
844-714-3454

Interior Image Credit: Amie Charney

ISBN: 979-8-3850-1152-0 (sc)
ISBN: 979-8-3850-1153-7 (hc)
ISBN: 979-8-3850-1154-4 (e)

Library of Congress Control Number: 2023921008

Print information available on the last page.

WestBow Press rev. date: 11/17/2023

WESTBOW
PRESS®
A DIVISION OF THOMAS NELSON
& ZONDERVAN

For my wonderful children
to read to my
future grandchildren, who
will be even
more wonderful.

Many people in Israel
grew tired and sad.
They'd waited so long
for a king to be had.

A Messiah, a Savior,
promised so long ago—
someone to help
bring joy
and new hope.

But a small stable boy
on a clear winter's night
sang to his lambs
with all of his might.

"God is always on time.
He's never late.
When we trust in Him,
it's worth the wait."

Three ancient wise men,
humble and bright,
looked into the heavens
and rejoiced at the sight.

A great star in the east
they would follow afar
to bring gifts for a king,
gold, frankincense,
and myrrh.

But when their path
was wearing or full of fright,
they sang to each other
with all of their might.

"God is always on time.
He's never late.
When we trust in Him,
it's worth the wait."

Sweet Mary and Joseph
were tired and weary.
The only room left
was a stable, so dreary.

Not really a place
to lay your head
or welcome new life
to a world full
of dread.

But when they held baby Jesus,
oh, what a sight!
They sang to their babe
with all of their might.

"God is always on time.
He's never late.
When we trust in Him,
it's worth the wait."

On a hillside not far
from where Jesus slept sweetly,
an angel appeared, saying,
"Shepherds, now heed me."

"Do not be afraid.
I come with great news.
In Bethlehem, your Savior was born.
He is Jesus, Messiah.
He is Christ the Lord."

Then, a whole host of angels
glowed with great light,
rejoicing and singing
with all of their might.

"God is always on time.
He's never late.
When we trust in Him,
it's worth the wait."

And now here **you** are,
A child of God,
redeemed and forgiven
and loved by the Lord.

Always remember
if sadness gets heavy,
when life feels hard,
or your questions
are many,

Jesus came to bring peace
and joy so bright.
So, rejoice, dance, and sing
with all of your might.

"God is always on time.
He's never late.
When we trust in Him,
it's worth the wait."

About the Author

Amie Charney is a mom, an author, and a teacher. She has lived and traveled the world on many fun adventures with her family, but now calls San Antonio, Texas home. She is always amazed by the stories you can create with only twenty-six letters in the alphabet (and a few sparkles of imagination). She used all the best letters and sparkles in this story, and hopes it will become a special part of your family's Christmas tradition.

Printed in the United States
by Baker & Taylor Publisher Services